The Phoenix Living Poets

A MAN IN WINTER

Poets Published in
The Phoenix Living Poets Series

★

JAMES AITCHISON

ALEXANDER BAIRD · ALAN BOLD

R. H. BOWDEN · FREDERICK BROADIE

GEORGE MACKAY BROWN

HAYDEN CARRUTH · JOHN COTTON

JENNIFER COUROUCLI

GLORIA EVANS DAVIES

PATRIC DICKINSON

TOM EARLEY · D. J. ENRIGHT

IRENE FEKETE

JOHN FULLER · DAVID GILL

PETER GRUFFYDD

J. C. HALL · MOLLY HOLDEN

JOHN HORDER · P. J. KAVANAGH

RICHARD KELL · LAURIE LEE

LAURENCE LERNER

CHRISTOPHER LEVENSON

EDWARD LOWBURY · NORMAN MACCAIG

ROY MCFADDEN

JON MANCHIP WHITE

JAMES MERRILL · RUTH MILLER

LESLIE NORRIS · ROBERT PACK

ARNOLD RATTENBURY

ADRIENNE RICH · JON SILKIN

JON STALLWORTHY

GILLIAN STONEHAM

EDWARD STOREY · TERENCE TILLER

SYDNEY TREMAYNE

LOTTE ZURNDORFER

A MAN IN WINTER

by

EDWARD STOREY

CHATTO AND WINDUS

THE HOGARTH PRESS

1972

Published by
Chatto and Windus Ltd
with The Hogarth Press Ltd
42 William IV Street
London W.C.2

*

Clarke, Irwin & Co. Ltd
Toronto

ISBN 0 7011 1855 5

Distributed in the United States of America
by Wesleyan University Press

ISBN 0 8195 7045 1

© Edward Storey 1972

Printed in Great Britain by
Lewis Reprints Ltd
London and Tonbridge

For Mary

Acknowledgements are made to *The Poetry Review; Anglo-Welsh Review; Critical Quarterly; Tribune; Countryman; B.B.C. East Anglia; Enigma; Scrip; Ariel* and *The Listener* for poems already printed and broadcast.

The author acknowledges assistance from the Arts Council of Great Britain.

CONTENTS

en Couple   9

vocation   10

arm-Hand   11

elery-Prickers   12

cceptance   13

ag-and-Bone-Man   14

ky Warning   15

Man in Winter   16

Ballad of Billy Blunt   17

ay   19

ound   20

he Dark Flower   21

he Dead and the Living   22

'ar Ends of Tired Days'   23

eace   24

ight   25

ou Too Had the Gift of Stars   26

ncle   27

eighbour   28

n Platform 5   29

Visit to the Valleys   30

irago?   31

aution   32

ight Psalm   33

Face in the Water   34

he Journey   35

FEN COUPLE

I see them again
brother and sister
sharing for seventy years
the same sad fire.

    Encamped in their damp
    corner of the room
    they watch their garden
    under perennial frost.

She could have done better,
letting fastidious hands
loose on a house.
But never with him.

    Content to stare
    at the starved grate
    he has spent his life
    twisting years round his thumbs.

And so they endure
eking care out like coal,
growing, in misery,
more in debt to each other.

INVOCATION

After a six month's death
I come to resurrect you for my own sake,
to put your flesh on to my raw nerves,
to shed the sophisticated fears
that have silenced this half year.
With these uncertain incantations now I come
to raise you out of the grave soil
until I stand as you, alone on the flat earth.

I come as always,
as a thought haunting the seasons of sleep,
as a shadow searching those fields
to which you mortgaged your bones.
Digging so long for my own crops
I have grown tired of their darkening acres,
have lost faith in the hands that once
clasped themselves into your safeguarding fingers.

I come because
you taught me once a certain fortitude,
held me close to the coarse cloth of your coat
until we and the land were as one —
you the unshakable, the reliable,
winter and sun, timber and stone.
Now more than ever I need your eyes
to look more wisely upon life's calendar.

Oh you my ghost
who could not write more than your name
yet walked the earth in an abundance of words
take me again into your arms
that I may return to my true task,
let me work daily in your shade
knowing that you laboured in your grief
using a bright spade for your song's pen.

ARM-HAND

would have portrayed you once
part of the rich character
f these fields, your ponderous limp
product of the black soil, the split
ots of your hands wealthy as muck.

would have dressed you in words
keep out the raw winds of your life,
ould have made you spectacular
the sun rising in winter, or as part
f a landscape by Breugel the elder.

ut that would have gilded
ur rank flower, would have disguised
e exhausted bud of your eyes
d silenced the loud ache
your bones' arthritis.

or someone's gain you have banged
ur head on a sky of indifference.
ou have grown old cursing the fields
r survival — a by-product of wealth
fying description.

CELERY-PRICKERS

You say too easily
there's virtue living near the soil.

Those women crawling on all-fours
pricking-out celery plants would not agree.

For them there is no comfort in a cold east wind
whipping their broad behinds all day.

Even the canvas screen around each bed
cannot protect them from the black wet earth.

The only profit they get from the land
comes once a week to fatten each tight purse.

Watching them from the comfort of a car
you might compare their stitchery of plants

with that more gentle art of tapestry,
seeking some finery that is not there.

But stand outside and feel their bawdy talk
suck that glib thought from your unseasoned roots.

ACCEPTANCE

Were you afraid of the first cockcrow
the first whipcrack of morning
snapping your bones out of an old mattress?

Were you afraid of the first footfall
the daybreak's inevitable knock
on the delicate pane of your dream's window?

Or were you glad when the sky's fist came
poking sleep out of your eyes
mocking the warmth of your threadbare blankets?

Were you relieved when the first birdsong
exploded your sleep releasing
your limbs from the love-sheets' arthritis?

I was glad. My incongruous bed
had bred many hungers. The indifference
of fields hurts less than a woman's.'

RAG-AND-BONE-MAN

This is where he lived
the rag-and-bone-man
who rifled my spare dreams.

In this yard he cursed
among bedsteads and fenders
the poor harvest of scrap

and thin autumn of brasses.
Chains rattled. Rain
rusted on mangles.

I remember his fence
and the walls of his shed
heavy with hare skins

among them the sad fur
of my own rabbit — killed
for our Sunday table —

its coat cold, the care
of my days strung up
for a few pence.

I hated that warped man
whose iron claws could
snatch from my small hands

the soft warmth of my pride
and give in return
the damp grief of his coins.

SKY WARNING

There is no reason why the sky should consider us
as it prepares for winter. We are not gods
to have control over the waiting snow
or wisdom over the fierce light of stars.

All day there has been a steady freezing of space
until the sky has become the colour of ice.
Black frost has clapped its padlock on the fields
sending the labourers home with stubborn hands.

And power-cables strung across the earth
grow taut beneath the arctic wind's broad bow,
their steel gut waiting for the first cold notes
to strike their chilling sounds into our pride.

A MAN IN WINTER

I think today of your inarticulate praising.
A man not concerned with the machinery of words,
content with nouns but not bothered with adjectives.

For you a lark singing through mist
was simply a lark, even though ice
clouded the air and the grass was frozen.

Sheep with rime caked on their backs
were just sheep who had grazed out all night
under frost that was perfectly natural.

And when the guttural croak of a pheasant
cracked over the water it was an echo
your ears took for granted. Washlands

flooded with winter were there for that purpose,
even though sunrise gave them miraculous colours
and pylons were stunned by their faultless reflections.

There was nothing fancy in your rejoicing,
no extraordinary phrases. Earth behaved
as you expected and for that you were grateful.

When I am no longer concerned
with the mechanics of language
this day will survive because of your eloquence.

A BALLAD OF BILLY BLUNT

(for Charles Causley)

We were always afraid of old Billy Blunt
with his gaiters, bowler and walking stick,
he was the terror and scourge of the town
and we seldom went near his house in the Walk.

His coat was as rough as a coalman's sack
his voice was as gruff as a concrete-mixer,
we were told that at night his house had a ghost
and the name of the ghost was 'Silas Marner'.

Sometimes on shadowy late afternoons
as we dawdled home from our C. of E. School
we'd spot old Billy coming towards us
and run for the nearest climbable wall.

Sometimes he would catch us all unaware
as we loitered about in St. Mary's Street —
'get out, get out of my way' he would growl
'get off the pavement and out of my sight'.

I never quite knew why we were afraid
or doffed our caps as the teachers taught,
for the figure who haunted our childhood then
was haunted by us in the end, I thought.

Yet we always stepped off the narrow path
when Billy went muttering on his way
with bright ball-bearings for his eyes
and a nose like the knot of a willow-tree.

Some nights when the moon shone over the Bower
and cobwebs were visible round his house,
we'd creep up as near as we possibly dare
to hear him counting the coins in his purse.

We knew he was rich as rich as a king
and as mean as a lonely millionaire;
on the night that he died he arose again
when a penny fell out of his coat on the chair.

Now Billy and Silas have long since gone,
and children now laugh as they go through the Walk,
though when I'm out walking alone in the streets
I think I still hear him tapping his stick.

'Get out, get out of my way' I hear
from the walls and pavements round Market Square,
and I know as I hurry back to my house
that old Billy's voice was the voice of fear.

And I hear people say and say many times
'we'll never have men like him anymore' —
and thank God for that I say to myself
as a penny rolls over my threadbare floor.

DAY

There is always this waiting
as the day unfolds itself
showing the fields still there
and cattle grazing at far intervals.

Something no doubt will spoil
the new-made promises.
Some word forced on the page,
some fearful thought meant to be lost in sleep.

Men pass my window
with more apparent ease than I
of starting each day's work,
as though their tasks have some fixed certainty.

I wait, hoping some hand
will move within my hand,
some small distraction come
to call me through the sky's inviting door.

As empty hours pass
and fields change leaf by leaf
there comes this late returning home
and evening's compromise.

FOUND

I heard a voice I thought I would not hear
   since that cold night and all the clanking stars
   locked out her music from my silent house.

Across the summer boundaries she came
   quite unexpectedly and filled my room
   with colours warmer than the ringing sun.

How could I keep her presence with me then,
   defying frost and midnight and the scorn
   outside my window of the prying dark.

Though voice was all that came across the air
   and silence rushed back in when sound was gone,
   my house glowed in the thought that she had been.

And though the night slunk in with stockinged-face
   and held a black-gloved hand across my eyes
   I knew that something lost we do not always lose.

THE DARK FLOWER

Always there is the same hunger.
However bright the day
or the acceptable letter
there is the heart's need
apparent even at daybreak.

I have tried the alternatives.
The intense pleasure of song
or a friend sharing
the mind's banquet.
But nothing satisfies.

The day's music is trivial.
The warm hands of strangers
are ephemeral. I hunger still
for the dark flower of love
that is imperishable.

THE DEAD AND THE LIVING

At Crowland it is easy to remember the dead.
Low sunlight lifts a stone-cross to your face.
Snow falls expectedly through the abbey's roof.

At this far end of day it is common to feel
sly shadows of long-boats darkening the Fens.
In low-lit seasons such hauntings are usual.

Stones here are cenotaphs — smashed columns that frame
a monotonous landscape. What they say
makes you think of the dead living under the dead.

I think today of those unknown living who died.
Armies that went down into a foreign desert.
Bones that rest now under chaotic airports.

I think of the dead where only the trees grow.
Where snow falls on long dismissed footprints.
Where no stones remember their ruined seasons.

I think of the unknown dead under today's living,
under new office blocks and expensive hotels,
under the roadways and new city pavements.

I think of those unliving faces of women
searching for looks in a junk-yard of mirrors.
Hiding their fears in a graveyard of wishes.

At Crowland it is easy to remember the living.
Snowlight brings your eyes down to a stone.
Under death's open roof we share the same epitaph.

'FAR ENDS OF TIRED DAYS' *Emily Dickinson*

Far off
like secret camp-fires burning in the night
patches of blazing cornstalk break the dark
singeing the shallow mist with streaks of smoke.

Cut off
from all the cold machinery of day
those flames could be the centre of deep thought,
of soldiers' plans and ancient heraldry.

Night waits.
The nostrils sniff again the earth-charred air
until from this quiet ridge above the fields
the mind hears bugles calling in the wind.

PEACE

This late light deepening on old stone
reminds me of a day's-end light on hills
where warmth was framed in complex distances.

Then I was new to all those shapes of rock
that changed with shadows on a map of cloud
stealing the far horizons from my sight.

But watching now this tall cathedral shine
I realise there was an equal calm
upon those wild and bright unsculptured heights.

These stones constructed to a plan
reclaim again their first identity —
earth back to earth beneath an ageing sun.

All is as one, reborn in evening light,
far hills, cathedral towers and peace,
renewing ancient stillness in this passing sky.

LIGHT

(for John Hutton)

All night I've coveted your painting of cool light,
envying the clear economy of line with which
you've fixed in shapes all that escapes my syllables.

There hung our common themes — bright water, space and sky —
reaching towards infinity where suns
are seen through webs of glass and green translucency.

Knowing the stillness of those waiting hours I asked
how were those ancient elements so truly caught,
how, out of chaos, was that peace restored?'

This morning as the darkness leaves my room
I stare into the resurrected day, still asking how
my hands might capture light in words of clay.

YOU TOO HAD THE GIFT OF STARS

(For Roye McCoye)

When you died
there were no usual announcements.
You could have fallen, alone,
on some advanced battlefield
with no messenger to wire back
news of your falling. Not even the comfort
of bewildered birds or the charred trees
mourning your burnt carcase.

Your death came
in its own peculiar silence —
a blind hand closing your nostrils,
your eyes returning their light to the sun.
Who could have known, in our far places,
that you lay in a white hospital
without life and among strangers;
aware no longer of our absences.

Hearing the news
some days later in a telephone kiosk
I could not trust the words that crackled
over towns and boundaries.
Staring at my dumb face in the glass
I stood beyond grief, ashamed that you —
the most genuine and companionable —
should have met death in your own company.

Walking away
from what had been a simple courtesy
I felt a vacuum split the earth and sky.
So Keats died, I thought, and Clare,
removed from their own kind.
To have known you was to have known
one of them. You too had the gift of stars
and shone in your own burning.

UNCLE

At last we have taken that picture down.
For more than twenty years his photograph
has looked out from our chimney-breast,
his calm, unblinking eyes watching us,
his regimental badge permanently bullshone.

As children we accepted his grey face
as part of the furniture, his fixed smile
hiding the fear of war — the khaki lie
of a young man nailed up on our wall,
pretending he was a soldier.

Three days later he was killed in France.
(Or was he drowned? I just forget.)
All I remember are the days of questioning,
the tears on faces I had not seen cry,
and then that blown-up photograph.

And now it's down what can we find
to put there in its place? A coloured print
of our own children and their wedding days?
Or something from our holiday in Wales?
Or shall we leave the nail for next year's calendar?

NEIGHBOUR

This neighbour-soldier found his death
in a delayed Flanders, with no sound
of shouting, bugles, gunfire.

After forty years nursing a proud wound
he died in a suburban house
rarely called on by friends or relations.

Rising to reveille he fell one day
and gashed his head upon the grate.
There was no witness, no trooper's comforting.

Lying stiff and bloody in his no-man's land
he did not hear the milkman slam the gate,
the postman shove a gas-bill through the door.

Police came, then cousins, and the corpse
was carted away like an old couch . . .
Since then the room's had many visitors.

watch you gripping your hands
that have grown into the familiar contours
of old age, waiting for the train
to begin its terrifying journey
back to yourself, to your small house
where the daily habit of being alone
will have to be learnt all over again.

Whatever you do with your lined face
nothing disguises that look in your eyes.
Between you and your family
words push like passengers until
your daughter kisses you goodbye —
uttering those parting platitudes
that spill about the closing of a door.

For them your visit's over and relief
jerks in the hands half-lifted now to wave.
Soon there will be far distances between
and duty letters counting out your year.
A whistle blows. The station moves away.
A magazine stays clenched upon your lap.
And your white knuckles tighten round each fear.

A VISIT TO THE VALLEYS

(for Bram)

I was a stranger
nurtured only on the long years of talk
about the steep slag-tips and those mountains
where after work the solitary miner climbed
to let the lark clear the dust from his ears
or the free hawk help him to forget the dark.

I had heard all about
those familiar landmarks of pit-heads and cages,
of trucks, lamp-rooms, and the sun-deprived faces.
They were all part of a saga interwoven with dreams,
with a strange nostalgia and traditional humour —
a mixture of pride in the coal-black gaul.

For me those valleys
were a scar on the breast of a country
where poor houses crouched in perennial shadows,
where blood bred with blood and the chapels
rang with relief rather than the real fervour of praise.
It was all, once, so much of a legend.

But now I have been,
and although most of the pit-heads are gone
and the tips and hillsides are bandaged with green,
I felt something of the old flavour, the fierce history
that raged under the pale flesh, the strength that made
even the unbearable partly acceptable.

I caught something
of the heart's inextinguishable warmth,
the character hacked out of the dark earth.
Taken at night through narrow streets to the colliery hall
I felt the depth of your true fire as my flesh glowed
by the released flames of your brass choir.

VIRAGO?

After the exaggeration about your fierce tongue
I was prepared for the claw-scratchings of your spite,
ready for the wrath and fire they said would pour
out of the sour volcano of your soul.

Then you came in, a forgotten cobweb
undisturbed in the world's mind for a hundred years,
no lava spilling from your mouth, no scorn,
only unspoken questions as we held your hands.

As we were carefully explained and named
I watched you thumb through albums of your brain
trying to recognise this woman who was child
in those starched-linen years where faces never change.

I watched you stare beyond the valley's rain
to where the fading coal-tips aged with moss,
sinking your shaft of thought deep down to understand
why I'd outgrown the age my mother was.

Poor ghost, poor fragile remnant of yellowing lace,
are you that wild virago of your family's talk?
If so they should come back to see you as you are,
your mind burnt out while theirs still blindly burn.

CAUTION

Legend has helped
to isolate this island.
Grey pebbled shores
    echo with violence,
    and the cold cliffs
are barbed with silence.

Lone cottages
spy out of valleys, their eyes
following strangers.
    Trees listen and hills
    record footsteps;
bleak fields are sinister.

On the dead beach
bleached bones grow whiter,
a prince's ghost
    troubles the water,
    and the black rocks
heave with suspicion.

History makes
the people live with caution.
They hold a secret
    no-one will discover;
    ask them the time
they will not even answer.

NIGHT PSALM

(for Barry Ferguson)

Here in this midnight are the stones of darkness,
under the towers of silence are the years of asking.

Beyond the echoes of prayer are the nightmares of labour,
in the sanctified roof are the forests of anger.

At this time there's no room for the temporal meaning,
in this precipitous minute we cannot fix history.

Your songs came from mouths that are no longer mortal,
you are already ghosts in a queen-haunted chancel.

Now each of us dwells in this infinite stillness
as effigies carved from its inaudible mystery.

The stones were erected here for this purpose,
for souls to be free of the passions that perish.

Sorrows before have come to these arches,
in this stretch of reverence is every tear's passing.

My eyes have felt grief at your late music's haunting,
my ribs have been crushed by the winter light's ending.

Wherever we go we are part of this darkness,
the stones hold us all like seeds in their crevices.

A FACE IN THE WATER

I search for you over the fields
knowing I'll never find you there.
I stand by the water and watch the ice
force your reflection to disappear.

I see a man ploughing up trees
buried for over three thousand years
beneath the sullen floods that came
before we'd learnt to sow our seeds.

I think of those secret woods
where we one winter ago
were buried alive in a season's love
that could not survive the spying snow.

What hand or machine will find
the words that we drowned then,
or plough for thoughts unborn by us
under the frozen heaven?

What time of year will it be
when some casual stranger comes
to stand by this ancient river
where the frost has hidden your eyes?

And who will he be I wonder,
what thoughts will he take home,
when your face re-appears in the water
and your secret lips stay dumb?

THE JOURNEY

One day we shall come to a hill
and after the charred city
find even the hill empty,

find nothing more
than the parched grass
and the paths worn by feet over the hill's back.

And we shall sit down
away from the dead pavement,
away from the disappeared highway,

and feel for the first time
the loss of passion;
the great darkness felt after our last loss.

There in silence we shall be free
not only to remember but to feel
how the sun shone before that noon-day of thunder.

We shall feel too how, even as children,
we stood helpless and crying,
our eyes scarred by a new fire.

And we shall be told then
'when you saw light
your waking light destroyed not you

but the little dreams within you;
your waking killed not evil
but all innocence'.

And to believe our ears
we'll rub our bones
into our wounded eyes,

into those gaping holes
where first light shone, and joy
ran through responsive flesh.

And all we thought was sleep
will be reality,
cold whiteness will consume our warmth
and freeze our comforts in unwilling thighs.

ii

Then halfway down the line
someone will say — Wait!
We have been here before.

This whiteness and the silence are familiar.
The snowy ash and shadows are as clear
as neon adverts in a brazen sky.

Somewhere we have seen before
these burnt-out symbols
and this charcoal cross.

Somewhere a sweet kiss left this sour moment
in our mouths and sultry fingers slyly pulled
a rope of fire round our necks.

Then slowly we shall be afraid,
not only of remembering
but of rediscovering that light

within our memory — that gentle light
we sadly found too searching,
too unbearable.

And without thinking,
without feeling our limbs moving,
we shall start walking.

Slowly,
Without speaking.
All of us walking together.

Pursued and led by the same memory.

iii

And after the first silence,
after the long darkness,
someone will start singing,

and others halfway down the line
will join in the singing;
not gay and robust songs

but quiet and nostalgic,
like the tired singing heard sometimes in a bus
on the return journey.

And we shall know then
that we must have felt stillness
deep in some ancient winter

when man fought against whiteness,
where eyes closed under the glare of light,
under that glare of winter.

And we shall know then that the songs
and the rhythms of walking
belong to an old sense,

that sometime, somewhere,
the same ordeal, the same fear,
had been gone through before,

only with more people.
And someone weeping
further down the line will say

'I can remember a time of great bleeding'.

iv

And after the song's ending,
after the generations of walking,
we shall come to a hill.

But the hill will be empty
or emptily haunted
like a park after curfew

or a theatre after a play
or an old dressing room
of a legendary actor.

And someone will say to himself
and not to his neighbour —
it was all playing,

playing and makebelieve,
singing and dancing,
a time of deception.

Who was it who spoke of
'the dark porch of eternity whence none returns
to tell the tale of his reception'?

He too was a man in winter.

v

So we have come to the hill,
and with stone eyes
stare out of our emptiness,

regretting we came too late,
regretting we came this far,
regretting the moment of birth,

regretting the day in the orchard,
regretting our knowledge of fire,
regretting the treason of language,

regretting perhaps
that we ever chose freedom
or walked out of summer.

Then out of our fears,
out of the tears that we cannot shed,
out of the battery-cells and mechanical heartbeat,

ut of the violence of civilization,
ut of the bloodshed of innocent children,
ut of the wounds exposed by each nation,

e'll feel our thighs twitching,
he human veins burning,
he great passions rising,

nd we shall rejoice
1 this new longing,
elieving, perhaps, that again

here is hope in the flesh,
n the genuine kiss,
n the birth of a seed.

nd somewhere, someday,
t the head of the line,
 child will call out —

Look! someone. I've found a flower'.

i

nd at the top of a hill
e shall see a great light
pread over the sky,

nd beyond that light
e shall smell lilies and meadowsweet,
alsam and honeysuckle.

nd our laments
ill explode into laughter,
to joy, shot out of singing,

to dancing, born out of darkness,
to children, born out of loving,
to life, born of our making.

nd we shall be free to return
ither to our grave silence, or to redeem
he true light of our ancient beginning.

9

For
after the charred city
and ruins of winter,

after the destruction
and uncountable casualties,
after the walk and the realization,

the hill of Golgotha is our hope.